Parent Shel
372.7

Anderson, Sally.
How many ways can you make
five?
2012.

Guad. Br.

Discarded by
Santa Maria Library

AUG 0 5 2013

D0942257

How Many Ways Can You Make Five?

A Parent's Guide to Exploring Math with Children's Books

BRANCH COPY

by Sally Anderson with the Vermont Center for the Book

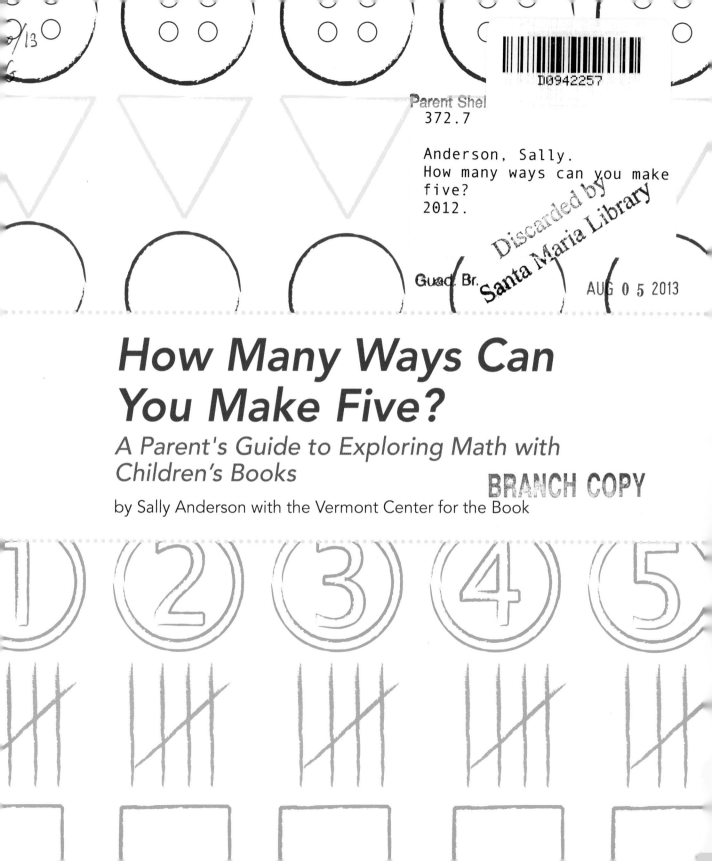

Also by Sally Anderson with the Vermont Center for the Book:

Social Studies and Me! Using Children's Books to Learn about Our World

Where Does My Shadow Sleep? A Parent's Guide to Exploring Science with Children's Books

Math & Science Investigations: Helping Young Learners Make Big Discoveries

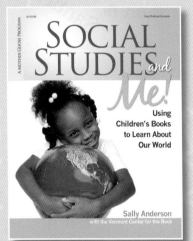

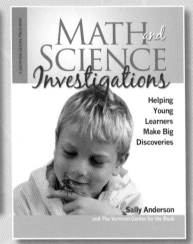

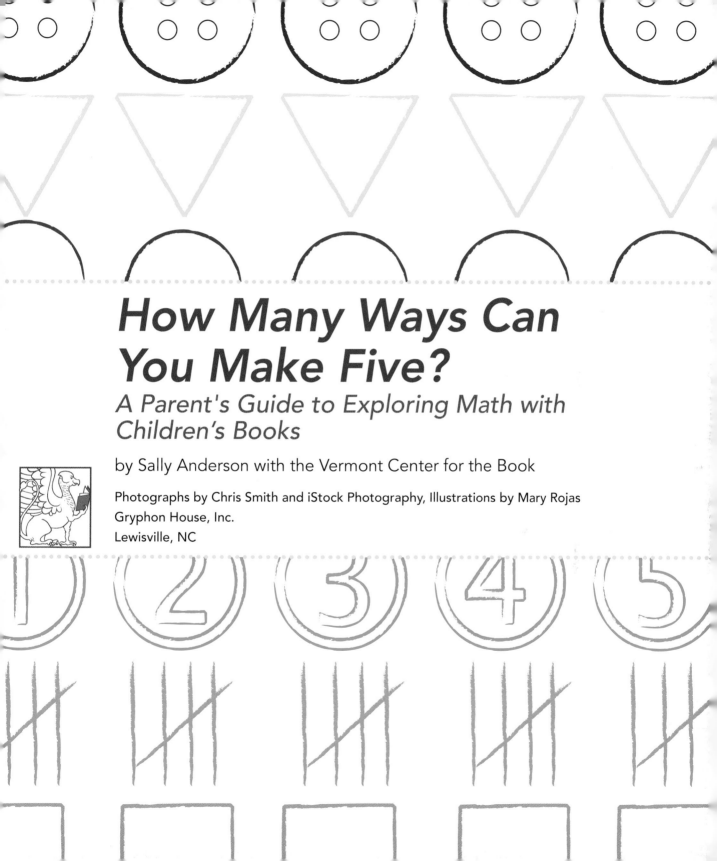

How Many Ways Can You Make Five?

A Parent's Guide to Exploring Math with Children's Books

by Sally Anderson with the Vermont Center for the Book

Photographs by Chris Smith and iStock Photography, Illustrations by Mary Rojas

Gryphon House, Inc.

Lewisville, NC

Bulk Purchase
Gryphon House books are available for special premiums and sales promotions as well as for fund-raising use. Special editions or book excerpts also can be created to specifications. For details, contact the Director of Marketing at Gryphon House.

Disclaimer
Gryphon House, Inc. cannot be held responsible for damage, mishap, or injury incurred during the use of or because of activities in this book. Appropriate and reasonable caution and adult supervision of children involved in activities, corresponding to the age and capability of each child involved, is recommended at all times. Do not leave children unattended at any time. Observe safety and caution at all times.

Copyright Sally Anderson with the Vermont Center for the Book ©2012

Published by Gryphon House, Inc.
PO Box 10, Lewisville, NC 27023
800.638.0928; 877.638.7576 (fax)

Visit us on the web at www.gryphonhouse.com.

All rights reserved. No part of this publication may be reproduced or transmitted in any form or by any means, electronic or technical, including photocopy, recording, or any information storage or retrieval system, without prior written permission of the publisher. Printed in the United States. Every effort has been made to locate copyright and permission information.

Cover photograph courtesy of iStock Photo, LP. All rights reserved. 2012. www.istockphoto.com.

Library of Congress Cataloging-in-Publication Data
Anderson, Sally.
 How many ways can you make five? : a parent's guide to exploring math with children's books / by Sally Anderson with the Vermont Center for the Book ; Illustrations by Mary Rojas.
     p. cm.
 Includes bibliographical references and index.
 ISBN 978-0-87659-386-8
 1. Mathematics--Study and teaching (Early childhood)--Activity programs.
 2. Children's literature in mathematics education. 3. Education--Parent participation. 4. Picture books for children--Educational aspects. I. Rojas, Mary, ill. II. Vermont Center for the Book. III. Title.
 QA19.L58A53 2012
 372.7--dc23
                                                2012004430

Table of Contents

0

Introduction

Children Love Math!

Why Use Children's Books to Talk about Math?

Math Is Everywhere, All the Time

Children Love Math!

Children love to figure things out, and math is a great tool for problem solving! Use this book to explore the world of mathematics with your child. Sit and read one or two of the suggested children's books, and then get up and do an activity together. As you have fun, your child will be learning about numbers, shapes, patterns, measuring, and lots more.

Young children use math concepts to investigate and understand their world by:

▶ Creating patterns using napkins, utensils, and dishes as they set the table for dinner;

▶ Counting and measuring while they help make a batch of cookies;

▶ Noticing that the structural features—windows, doors—of their bedrooms contain more squares than triangles;

▶ Sorting and re-sorting their collections of toy cars, using different attributes each time; and

▶ Lining up their stuffed animals on the shelf from smallest to biggest.

Why Use Children's Books to Talk about Math?

Stories are a powerful way to introduce mathematics. Researchers recommend using children's picture books to develop math skills and understanding, because children's books can:

▸ Provide a story context for mathematics content;

▸ Suggest manipulatives for a variety of math investigations;

▸ Encourage children to re-create stories in their own way, as well as to practice math skills;

▸ Suggest problems that can be solved using different strategies: *How could we sort the laundry? How can we use these blocks to build a castle?*

▸ Develop math concepts such as mapping, following directions, and finding shapes in the environment;

▸ Encourage the use of math language: *How many? How far? How much?*

▸ Help children make sense of their world.

Many wonderful children's books easily lend themselves to the discussion of math concepts. For example, when you read one of the many versions of the story *The Three Billy Goats Gruff*, you can act out the story together using positional and directional words such as *over, under, near, beneath,* and *behind;* you can talk about the concept of *three;* you can learn about ordinal words such as *first, next,* and *last.*

How Many Ways Can You Make Five? was developed for children ages four and older, but most of the activities also work well with younger children. *How Many Ways Can You Make Five?* will help you and your child have fun reading about, talking about, and exploring math in your everyday lives

Reading to and with your child is a great idea! Children's books engage your little one, opening a door to the joys of imagination. In addition, your child has a natural curiosity about numbers: *How many? How high? How long? Which is bigger? Which weighs more?* Exploring math concepts provides benefits to your child for a lifetime. But using children's books to talk about math? Yes! You'll be amazed at the ways your child begins to notice and make connections with numbers in everyday life.

Math Is Everywhere, All the Time

Reading books to your child and talking about math helps your child see all the connections between math and what he or she does every day.

Reading Together

▶ Borrow or buy books that have explicit math content such as counting and measuring. There are lots of counting books to choose from: *1 ,2, Buckle My Shoe* by Anna Grossnickle Hines or *Ten, Nine, Eight* by Molly Bang are just two suggestions. More books are listed in the bibliography.

- Read books that have repeated sequences of events. Point out the events, and give your child an opportunity to make a prediction by asking, *What happens next?* Books about routines, such as the classic *Froggy Gets Dressed* by Jonathan London or *10 Minutes till Bedtime* by Peggy Rathmann, are fun to read.
- Look for math words and concepts in all picture books.
- Make connections between shapes in books and shapes in the environment.
- Talk about the problems the characters in a book are solving. Brainstorm other suggestions for solving those problems.

Talking Together

- Use appropriate math vocabulary such as:
- Sequence: *What comes first? What's next?*
- Shape: *Is that sign a square?* and
- Number names.
- Wonder aloud about *more than* and *less than* and *same as* or *equal to*.
- Look for and talk about numbers you find in your environment.
- Look for and describe patterns in the environment both indoors and outdoors: on book covers, on clothing, in a garden, on buildings.
- Record the outdoor temperature daily. When discussing this information, use words that show a comparison, such as *colder than*, *warmer than*, and *the same as*.
- Encourage your child to use directional and positional language, such as *up, down, near, over, under, beneath,* and *behind*.
- Use everyday situations to promote mathematical thinking, for example: *How many plates will we need when we set the table for dinner? How is this red marker the same as that red crayon? How is it different?*

- Help your child notice patterns of objects, colors, shapes, and words.
- Help your child make simple counting books.
- Help your child make drawings, charts, and models that show what he or she understands about math.

How Many Ways Can You Make Five? offers suggestions to help you and your child explore math in your everyday lives. Select the information, activities, and explorations in this book that appeal to you and your child. Some of the activities can be explored over several days, while others are shorter and can be enjoyed over and over again.

Math in Your Home

It's easy to incorporate math into your everyday routine.

- Have standard and nonstandard measuring tools available. You and your child can use a standard measuring tool, such as a ruler, to measure how many inches tall a chair is, or you can use a nonstandard measuring tool, such as a paper clip, to decide how big your child's favorite doll is.
- Let your child use a computer to explore mathematical concepts. Search for websites that offer age-appropriate activities. Evaluate software by checking reviews that appear in the mainstream media or information published by reputable organizations such as Parents' Choice Foundation (www.parents-choice.org) or Common Sense Media (www.commonsensemedia.org).

- ▶ Provide materials that encourage math exploration: unit blocks, parquetry blocks or tangrams, collections of small objects, containers to fill and empty.
- ▶ Provide objects (toys, paper clips, buttons) for counting, comparing, measuring, and sorting.

Because our world is filled with patterns, shapes, sequences, and numbers—all of which are math concepts—math is all around us. Young children naturally learn these math concepts through play and interactions with the adults in their lives. Use the ideas in this book as a springboard for enjoying the world of mathematics with your child.

1

Much More than Counting

Much More than Counting

When children explore numbers and learn to count, they begin to develop *number sense,* an understanding of the different uses for numbers. They also learn the sequence of numbers (as well as how to count backward). Young children explore addition and subtraction by counting groups of objects, by recognizing how many in a set (group) of objects, and by understanding terms such as *more than* and *less than.*

Every day there are opportunities to discover more about numbers and counting:

▶ Count how many cookies on the plate, books borrowed from the library, or chairs at the table.

▶ Separate a bag of groceries into groups (sets), and count how many in each group.

▶ Talk about *more than* and *less than* as you put away toys, laundry, and so on.

▶ Look for and name written numerals in books, around your home, in stores, and everywhere you go.

Reading picture books and doing hands-on math activities are wonderful ways to spend time with your child. In addition to having fun, you will be developing your child's understanding of math concepts and skills as you ask open-ended questions and encourage her to explain what she is doing. To reinforce your child's learning, provide many experiences with the same number or operation, such as doing many different activities using one number, or making and counting sets using a variety of different materials.

Books

There are lots of books about numbers and counting! Here are just a few suggestions. Ask y our public librarian for more suggestions or visit your local bookstore.

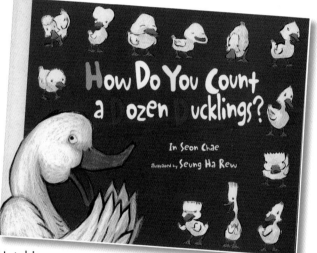

10 Minutes till Bedtime by Peggy Rathmann

12 Ways to Get to 11 by Eve Merriam

The Doorbell Rang by Pat Hutchins

How Do You Count a Dozen Ducklings? by In Seon Chae

How Many How Many How Many by Rick Walton

Quack and Count by Keith Baker

Ten, Nine, Eight by Molly Bang

Reading Tips

Remember that reading a picture book is a great way to spend time together. As you talk about each page, ask your child open-ended questions that will prompt a conversation rather than a simple yes-or-no answer. Here are some examples:

- ▸ *What does that remind you of?*
- ▸ *What do you notice about this character that reminds you of someone you know?*
- ▸ *What do you notice about...?*
- ▸ *What is the character doing?*
- ▸ *How many...?*
- ▸ *How much...?*
- ▸ *How heavy...?*
- ▸ *What do you think about...?*
- ▸ *Can you explain that?*
- ▸ *What makes that happen?*

Here are some mathematical terms you will find in the activities that follow. The most important thing that you will be helping your child develop is *number sense,* which is all about understanding the different uses for numbers.

- ▸ *One-to-one correspondence:* Counting each object only once is a verbal–object-counting skill. Most children develop this skill at age three or four.
- ▸ *Part-part-whole:* Recognizing part-part-whole relationships (putting numbers together and taking them apart) is a basic part of developing number sense. For example, two plus three equals five, and four plus one also equals five.
- ▸ *Set:* A collection or group of items.
- ▸ *Numeral:* The written symbol referring to a number. Most children develop an understanding of numerals between the ages of three and six.

Children may begin counting out loud as early as age two, although very young children often say the numbers out of sequence or with some numbers missing. Most kindergarteners are able to count in a continuous sequence from one to ten and to understand one-to-one correspondence.

It's easy to figure out what your child knows about numbers. Hold up three fingers and ask, "How many fingers am I holding up?" or "Can you touch each finger and count my fingers?" Now ask your child to hold up three fingers. Touch and count each finger. If you hold up five fingers, can your child touch and count them? eight fingers? ten?

Begin with the activities in this chapter that match or strengthen your child's number sense and knowledge of numbers, and then help her expand her understanding and knowledge by selecting activities that are more challenging for her.

I Know 3, Three,

Learn to count an object only once, using one-to-one correspondence, beginning with the number *three*.

Great Books to Read Before Doing This Activity

How Many How Many How Many by Rick Walton
Ten, Nine, Eight by Molly Bang
The Three Bears by Paul Galdone

What's Needed

markers
small objects such as buttons, stickers, crayons, and paper clips
small paper plates
yarn or string (for making loops)

How to Do It

1. Talk with your child about the number three. Can you think of nursery rhymes or stories that feature three characters? (The stories "The Three Little Kittens," "The Three Little Pigs," and "Goldilocks and the Three Bears" all feature three characters.) Mention other words that designate three: *trio, triplet,* and so on.

2. Explore the materials. How many different ways can you make three? Try making different groups of three objects.

3. Use the yarn or string to make loops on the floor or a table. Place each group of three objects in a loop.

4. Help your child write the numeral *3* on one paper plate and the word *three* on another paper plate.

5. Take turns counting the objects in each loop, and then put those objects on one of the two paper plates.

6. When your child is ready to count higher, choose another number and repeat the activity.

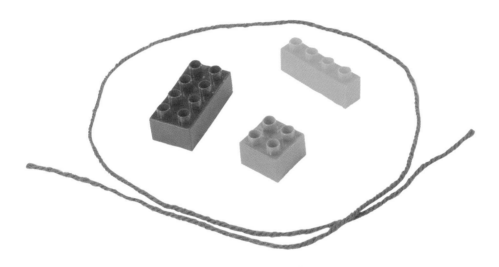

Build a Number Creature

Recognize *how many* in a set of objects as you build a number creature.

Great Books to Read Before Doing This Activity

1, 2, Buckle My Shoe by Anna Grossnickle Hines

Feast for 10 by Cathryn Falwell

Fish Eyes by Lois Ehlert

What's Needed

collage materials, such as cut-out paper shapes, stickers, craft feathers,
toothpicks, craft sticks, chenille sticks, and yarn

glue sticks

one number die

paper towel tubes

scissors

tape

How to Do It

1. Use a paper towel tube for the base. The tube can be used horizontally or vertically to create a "creature."

2. Roll the die and, whatever number comes up, choose that many of each collage material.

3. Create your creature by attaching the materials to the tube base. For example, if you rolled a four, you might attach four feathers for wings, four strips of paper for stripes, four stickers for eyes, and so on. Be creative!

4. Help your child name his creature (incorporating the number in the creature's name, such as Four-Feathered Fred), and then make a label for the creature.

(Adapted from NCTM's *Showcasing Mathematics for the Young Child*, 2004.)

Count and Match Sets

Make sets of objects, count how many objects are in each set, learn the sequence of numbers, then create matching sets of the same number.

Great Books to Read Before Doing This Activity

12 Ways to Get to 11 by Eve Merriam
Five Creatures by Emily Jenkins
Seven Blind Mice by Ed Young

What's Needed

cards or small paper plates with a numeral written on each (for matching)
crayons or markers
objects for counting (blocks, buttons, small toys)
paper

How to Do It

1. Explore, talk about, and count the various objects you and your child have collected.

2. Show your child how the objects can be counted and arranged in a set. Make and count sets of three. As you make a set, ask your child:

   ▸ *How many objects are in this set? How do you know?*

   ▸ *Can you use different objects to make a new set that matches the number of objects in my set?*

   ▸ *Can you show me the numeral that matches this set?*

3. Select another number and make your own set. Ask your child to make up her own, and then match each other's sets. Again, ask your child:

   ▸ *How many objects are in this new set? How do you know?*

   ▸ *Can you use different objects to make your own set that matches the number of objects in my set?*

   ▸ *Can you show me the numeral that matches this set?*

4. Make drawings of your sets. Help your child write the appropriate numeral on each drawing.

5. Repeat this activity many times, using bigger numbers as your child learns to touch and count each object once (1 paper clip, 2 paper clips, 3 paper clips, and so on). This is called *one-to-one correspondence,* an important math concept.

Count to Five Book

Make a book about counting to five, and recognize and name written numerals.

Great Books to Read before Doing This Activity
Five for a Little One by Chris Raschka
Five Little Monkeys Jumping on the Bed by Eileen Christelow
Hippos Go Berserk! by Sandra Boynton

What's Needed
blank book or several sheets of paper folded in half and stapled together
    along the crease
markers or crayons

How to Do It
1. Talk with your child about counting books.
2. Read one or two counting books together (see the list of suggestions).
3. Help your child notice that each number in the book is represented by a set of objects, for example: 1, one blueberry; 2, two cats. Ask her, *What comes next?*
4. Tell your child you are going to help her make her own counting book.
5. Help your child decide which objects she would like to use to illustrate each number in her own counting book.
6. Let your child do as much of the work as she can. Help by offering ideas and encouragement if needed.

7. You may want to take several days to complete the book. After the book is completed, share it with family members or friends.

8. Older children might want to make a counting book up to a higher number or a book counting by 2s, 5s, or 10s, up to 100.

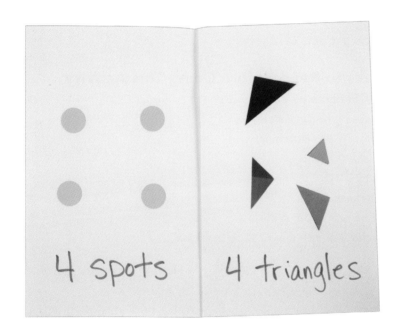

Count and Match Numerals

Recognize *how many* in a set of objects by making a set of cards to mix and match numerals and sets of objects.

Great Books to Read Before Doing This Activity
10 Minutes till Bedtime by Peggy Rathmann
Counting Kisses by Karen Katz
Ten Red Apples by Pat Hutchins

What's Needed
crayons or markers
index cards or small paper plates
magazines, scissors, and glue or tape (optional)
stickers

How to Do It
1. Make two sets of cards with your child. One set will have the numerals *1* through *5* on the cards. The other set will have pictures of objects (dots, triangles, balls, and so on) in groups of one through five.
2. To make the second set of cards, help your child place stickers on the index cards, draw pictures on them, or cut pictures out of magazines and glue or tape them on index cards.
3. Play a matching game with the cards. Find the numeral card that matches each picture-set card.

4. Older children may be able to find two cards that equal one card. For example, the picture cards for *two* and *three* could be put together to match a numeral 5 card. Or the numeral cards for *1* and *2* could be matched with the picture card for *three*.

5. Try this activity using other playing cards or dominoes.

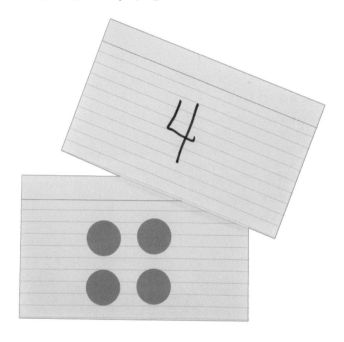

Fix My Mistake!

Use your number cards to help your child learn the sequence of numbers.

Great Books to Read Before Doing This Activity
Anno's Counting Book by Mitsumasa Anno
One Duck Stuck by Phyllis Root
Ten Little Fish by Audrey Wood

What's Needed
playing cards or the numeral cards from Count and Match Numerals on pages 28–29

How to Do It
1. Start with the cards for numerals *1*, *2*, and *3*. One player lays out the cards in a mixed-up order.
2. The player who has laid out the cards says, "Fix my mistake."
3. The other player puts the cards in the correct order. For example:

4. With practice, your child will be able to play this game with more numbers or with a series of numbers that does not start with one. For example:

Have fun playing Go Fish! This game and other card games give children practice counting groups of objects.

Directions for Go Fish!

1. Remove the face cards (aces, jacks, queens, kings) if you are using a regular deck of cards.

2. Each player gets five cards, and the rest are put in the center as the "pond."

3. The goal is to collect sets of two cards of the same number. (Experienced players can try to collect sets of four cards of the same number.)

4. One player asks another player for cards that she needs. For example, "Amy, do you have any fives?" If Amy has any of the cards requested, she must give all of them to the player who asked the question.

5. When Amy does not have any of the cards requested, she says, "Go fish," and the player who asked the question draws a card from the "pond."

6. Any time a player gets what she needs (either from another player or from the "pond"), she gets another turn.

   Hint: *Young children often have difficulty holding several cards in their hands at once. Your child may need to lay down her matches as she makes them.*

7. If a player runs out of cards, she draws five cards from the "pond."

8. The game ends when there are no more cards in the "pond." The player with the most sets is the winner.

Making Sets of Five

Begin to understand addition by counting and creating groups of objects.

Great Books to Read Before Doing This Activity

Apple Countdown by Joan Holub
How Many How Many How Many by Rick Walton
We All Went on Safari by Laurie Krebs

What's Needed

crayons
paper
pompoms (or other small, soft objects)
string or yarn to create circles

How to Do It

1. With your child, make a string or yarn circle on the floor.

2. Count out five pompoms and drop the pompoms one by one into the circle. Note: Soft objects work best because they will not roll so far away when dropped. Look at and talk about what you notice:

    ▸   *How many are inside the circle?*

    ▸   *How many are outside the circle?*

    ▸   *Do you still have five pompoms? Let's count them. Three outside the circle plus two inside the circle equals...?*

3. Try this several times, asking the same questions. Talk about *more than, less than,* and *equal to.*

4. Make drawings of where the pompoms land in the circle. Talk about inside sets (how many pompoms land inside the circle) and outside sets (how many pompoms land outside the circle).

5. Try this with eight or ten pompoms.

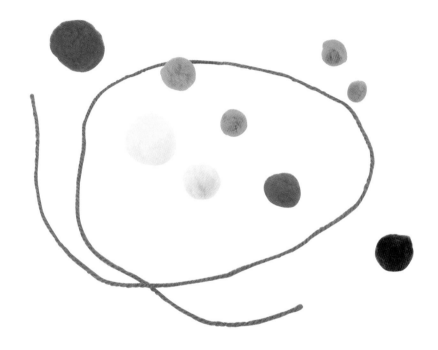

How Many Ways Can We Make Seven?

Discover ways to make seven, and begin to develop an understanding of addition by putting together and taking apart numbers.

Great Books to Read Before Doing This Activity
12 Ways to Get to 11 by Eve Merriam
How Do You Count a Dozen Ducklings? by In Seon Chae
Quack and Count by Keith Baker

What's Needed
seven objects, such as buttons, paper clips, or small blocks

How to Do It
1. Count aloud to make sure you have seven objects.
2. Experiment and talk about some ways you can arrange the objects in sets that would equal seven.
3. Work together making different combinations of sets using the seven objects. How many different ways can you make seven?

4. Make and label drawings of some of your sets.
5. Try this with nine or ten objects.

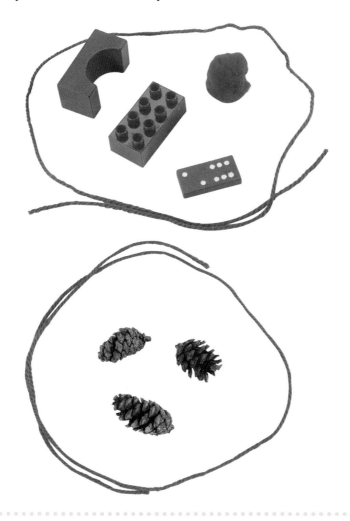

Symbols such as plus (+), minus (−), and equals (=) are called *function signs.*

I Can Add!

Practice simple addition as you begin to make number sentences (equations) with concrete objects and written numerals.

Great Books to Read Before Doing This Activity

How Many Snails? by Paul Giganti, Jr.
Over in the Meadow by Ezra Jack Keats
Quack and Count by Keith Baker
Ten Red Apples by Pat Hutchins

What's Needed

index cards and pieces of paper
marker
small objects such as blocks, dominoes, game pieces, or buttons
small squares of paper or index cards showing + (plus) and = (equals) signs

How to Do It

1. Ask your child to line up five blocks on a piece of paper. Ask, *Can you arrange these blocks in two sets that will equal five?*

2. Work together to make sets of two and three, one and four, and so on.

3. Now, you are ready to make addition number sentences (equations) that add up to five! Place two blocks on the table, and ask your child to count them out loud.

4. After your child counts the blocks, place the plus (+) card to the right of the two blocks and ask, *How many blocks should I add to make five blocks?*

5. Have your child count the blocks, then put the equals (=) card to the right of the blocks and count out five more blocks. As you point to the blocks, say, *Two blocks plus three blocks equals five blocks.* Ask your child to point and say the same words.

6. Help your child make numeral cards with the index cards and marker, and then help her match the correct numerals to the blocks in the number sentence.

7. Work together to make different number sentences. Help your child place the function cards in the right places and say the number sentences out loud.

8. Repeat this many times with different objects and numbers, allowing your child to make the number sentences and match the numerals.

Try Subtraction!

Addition leads to subtraction! Begin to understand subtraction by counting a group of objects, then "taking away" a few objects and counting again.

Great Books to Read Before Doing This Activity
10 Minutes till Bedtime by Peggy Rathmann
Bunny Money by Rosemary Wells
The Doorbell Rang by Pat Hutchins

What's Needed
index cards and pieces of paper
marker
small objects such as blocks, paper clips, or buttons
small squares of paper showing – (minus) and = (equals) signs

How to Do It
1. Ask your child to line up five blocks on a piece of paper. Together, count the five blocks out loud.
2. Take away two blocks and count how many remain.
3. Now create a number sentence. Line up the five blocks again, and place a minus (–) card to the right of the five blocks. Say, *Five blocks minus. . .*
4. Place two blocks to the right of the minus (–) card. Ask your child to remember how many blocks will be left if two blocks are taken away, or subtracted, from the five blocks. (Review step 2 if necessary.) Add the equals (=) card and then three blocks. Say, *Five blocks minus two blocks equals three blocks. You have created a number sentence or* equation. *You have* subtracted *two from five.*

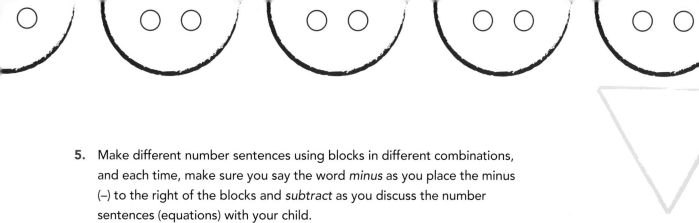

5. Make different number sentences using blocks in different combinations, and each time, make sure you say the word *minus* as you place the minus (–) to the right of the blocks and *subtract* as you discuss the number sentences (equations) with your child.

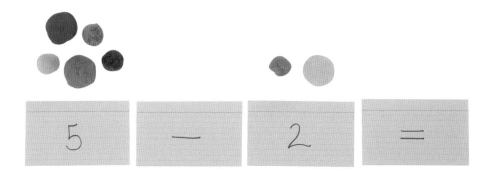

2

Shapes and Spaces

Shapes and Spaces

Understanding geometry begins with recognizing, naming, and manipulating shapes, and observing and describing shapes and objects in the environment. Early geometry experiences help children describe, measure, build, and classify the world around them.

Here are some examples of how you and your child can explore shapes and spaces:

- ▶ Find the right shape for a space in a puzzle.
- ▶ Put block shapes together to make new shapes and create designs.
- ▶ Locate circles in the supermarket.
- ▶ Observe that one room is larger than another room.
- ▶ Describe and identify the attributes of shapes, such as number of sides, corners, or faces.
- ▶ Tell each other how to find something or how to get somewhere.

Your child will learn about shapes and spaces through hands-on experiences and by talking about what he observes and knows and understands about the environment.

Books

A Circle Here, A Square There by David Diehl
Grandfather Tang's Story by Ann Tompert
The Shape of Things by Dayle Ann Dodds
Shapes That Roll by Karen Nagel
The Wing on a Flea by Ed Emberley

Reading children's books together can extend your child's math knowledge. Almost any picture book offers opportunities to search for and talk about shapes and spaces. The illustrations in children's books feature shapes in many different contexts, and any book about a trip will lead to good discussions using positional words! Acting out stories and poems is another way to practice those same skills.

Concept books such as *Shapes, Shapes, Shapes* by Tana Hoban are fun to look at over and over with your child. Ellen Stoll Walsh's *Mouse Shapes* shows many creative ways shapes can be used in illustrations.

One way to introduce and talk about spaces is to use a concept book such as *Me on the Map* by Joan Sweeney. Like many concept books, you will want to look at and read just one or two spreads at different times and make connections to the other books you have read to your child. For example, after you have looked at the house map featured in *Me on the Map*, look at some of the maps in Sara Fanelli's *My Map Book*. How are maps the same in each book? How are they different? If you wanted to draw a map of Hetty's walk in *Down the Road*, what would it look like?

Location and Direction Words

Use these words with your child as you talk about position, location, and direction:

on, off

on top of, under

top, bottom

in front of, behind

next to, between

up, down

forward, backward, sideways

around, through

near, far

close to, far from

Shapes All Around

Locate and name shapes in the environment, and describe their locations by using positional words, such as *over, under, near, beneath,* and *behind.*

Great Books to Read Before Doing This Activity

Round Is a Mooncake by Roseanne Thong

The Shape of Things by Dayle Ann Dodds

Shapes, Shapes, Shapes by Tana Hoban

What's Needed

collection of block shapes or paper shapes (circles, triangles, squares, rectangles, diamonds, and other geometric shapes)

How to Do It

1. Have your child select one shape (such as a rectangle), and talk together about this shape. Ask questions such as the following:
   - ▸ *What do you notice about the shape?*
   - ▸ *How many sides does it have?*
   - ▸ *What is it called?*
   - ▸ *Can you draw this shape in the air?*
   - ▸ *Can you make it larger in the air?*
   - ▸ *Can you make the shape with your body?*

2. Look around the room and search for objects, such as a table, or features, such as windows or doors, that are rectangles. You will be surprised at how many you can find!

3. Talk about what is the same or different about the rectangles you find.

4. Help your child make a drawing of the shape you identified (rectangle) and one or more of the objects you found.

5. At other times, repeat this activity with each geometric shape.

Shape Walk

Name, describe, compare, draw, and sort shapes that you discover all around your home or neighborhood.

Great Books to Read Before Doing This Activity
Every Friday by Dan Yaccarino
Knuffle Bunny by Mo Willems
Museum Shapes by the Metropolitan Museum of Art
Shapes, Shapes, Shapes by Tana Hoban

What's Needed
a paper or block shape to carry with you

How to Do It
1. Select one shape to search for, and bring it with you on your walk.
2. Go for a shape walk around your home or neighborhood.
3. When you see a shape, describe its position to your child: *I see a rectangle! It's next to the front door of that house, above the flower box.*
4. Encourage your child to talk about the shape as well.
5. Compare the shapes you find with the example you are carrying with you.
6. After you have searched for one particular shape a number of times, go on a shape search to find as many different shapes as you can.

7. Make a list of the shapes you see during your walk, and when you return, make a tally chart of your findings. Ask, *How many squares did we find? How many circles did we find? What does our tally chart tell us about what we found?*

    Hint: Making a tally chart is another important math skill: collecting data.

8. Continue to talk about the shapes you see when you take a walk or travel by bus or car.

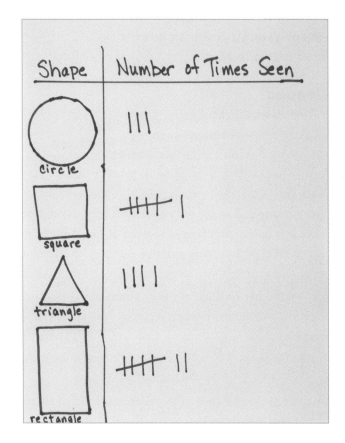

What's This Shape?

Observe, identify, and describe characteristics of shapes, using math language relating to shapes and spaces such as shape names, size words, positional words, and so on.

Great Books to Read Before Doing This Activity

Shape by Shape by Suse MacDonald
The Shape of Things by Dayle Ann Dodds
Shapes That Roll by Karen Nagel

What's Needed

box or bag in which to hide shapes
collection of block shapes or paper shapes (circles, triangles, squares, rectangles, diamonds, and other geometric shapes)

How to Do It

1. Spread your shape collection out on a table. Sort the collection by shape. As you sort and name each shape, talk about its attributes (characteristics). Encourage your child to use descriptive words such as *number* of sides, *longer than* and *shorter than*, *straight* or *curved* edges, and so on.

2. Challenge each other to think of things some of the shapes could be, such as, *Four circles are like the tires on a car*, or *Five squares in a row look like the sidewalk*.

3. Play What's This Shape? Have your child put one of each shape in your box or bag.

4. Take turns putting your hands in to select and touch a shape. Without taking the shape out of the bag and without looking, try to identify the shape. How can you tell what it is without looking? *It has curved sides—it's a circle!*

Making Shapes

Predict and test the ways shapes can be combined or taken apart to make other shapes and patterns.

Great Books to Read Before Doing This Activity
Shape by Shape by Suse MacDonald
A Star in My Orange by Dana Meachen Rau
The Wing on a Flea by Ed Emberley

What's Needed
variety of shapes in many sizes, cut out of paper

How to Do It
1. Place several squares in front of you. How many different ways can you make new, bigger squares?
2. *What other shapes can you combine to make a square?* Talk about which shapes and how many shapes you used to make the squares.
3. Make a rectangle: *What shapes can you combine to make a rectangle? What shapes did you use?*
4. Make a hexagon: *What shapes can you combine to make a hexagon? What shapes did you use?*
5. Try using a hexagon as a base and putting other shapes on top of it like filling in a puzzle.

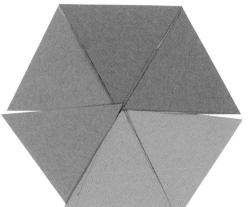

Shape Picture

Notice what changes when shapes are flipped or turned, and compare shapes that are different sizes.

Great Books to Read Before Doing This Activity

A Circle Here, A Square There by David Diehl
I Spy Shapes in Art by Lucy Micklethwait
The Shape of Things by Dayle Ann Dodds

What's Needed

crayons or markers
paper
shapes

How to Do It

Just One Shape

1. Together, decide which shape you would like to use.

2. Try out various ways one shape, drawn in different sizes and arranged in different ways, can be used to make a one-shape picture: a town made out of triangles, a spaceship from diamonds, a room from rectangles, and so on.

3. Help your child create a one-shape picture. Talk together about the many ways just one shape can be changed: It can be small, big, thin, wide, elongated, and so on.

All the Shapes

1. Create pictures using as many different geometrical shapes as possible.
   How many different shapes did you use in your picture?

2. Count all of the shapes in your picture. *How many did you use altogether?*

Shape Collages

Make shape collages and talk about them using math language relating to shapes and spaces, such as shape names, size words, positional words, and so on.

Great Books to Read Before Doing This Activity

Mouse Shapes by Ellen Stoll Walsh
Shape Space by Cathryn Falwell
Shapes, Shapes, Shapes by Tana Hoban

What's Needed

glue
magazines and other sources of pictures
paper
scissors

How to Do It

1. Decide which shape you want to explore.

2. Find and cut out examples of the shape from your magazines and other sources.

3. Glue the shapes to the paper to make a shape collage.

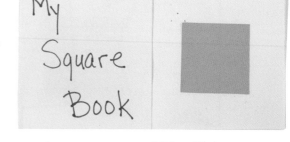

4. Make *My Shape Book*. Select a shape and encourage your child to fill the pages of a blank book with pictures of different objects illustrating that shape. The pictures can be cut from magazines or drawn by your child. The book itself could be made in the same shape! For example, rectangle-shaped pieces of paper for *My Rectangle Book*, paper plates for *My Circle Book*, and so on.

Triangle Block Puzzle

Make squares by moving, flipping, and combining triangles. Predict and test the ways shapes can be combined or taken apart in order to make other shapes and patterns.

Great Books to Read Before Doing This Activity

The Quilting Bee by Gail Gibbons
Quilting Now and Then by Karen Bates Willing and Julie Bates Dock
Sweet Clara and the Freedom Quilt by Deborah Hopkinson

What's Needed

6" x 6" piece of construction paper
four 3" x 3" pieces of construction paper (a different color from the base)

How to Do It

1. Fold each 3" x 3" piece of paper diagonally, and cut along the folds to make eight triangles

2. Put the 6" x 6" piece of paper down to use as a base.

3. Ask, *Will one of the triangles fit on this square?* and have your child place one of the triangles on the square. *Can you find another place where a triangle will fit on the square?*

4. Working together, talk about and try all the different ways the triangles can be placed on the 6" square.

5. As your child arranges triangles, have him move the triangles around, fitting them together on the square like a puzzle.
   Hint: Allow a lot of time for trial and error!

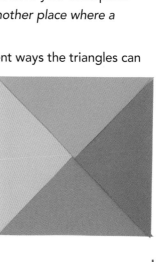

6. You and your child will want to do this activity many times.

7. Challenge other family members and friends to solve the Triangle Block Puzzle.

Explore Tangrams

Tangrams begin with a square that is cut into seven standard pieces. Each piece is called a *tan*. In creating a picture, all seven pieces (or tans) must be used. They must touch, but none may overlap.

Great Books to Read Before Doing This Activity

Grandfather Tang's Story by Ann Tompert
Three Pigs, One Wolf, and Seven Magic Shapes by Grace Maccarone
The Warlord's Puzzle by Virginia Pilegard

What's Needed

two tangram sets, one for each of you

Make Your Own Tangram Sets

You can find patterns to make your own sets on the Internet, and there are many interactive websites with tangram resources. Use the keywords *tangram patterns for kids* to find information, patterns, and games. The following are a few we recommend from the many available:

http://tangrams.ca/inner/diver.htm

http://pbskids.org/sagwa/games/tangrams/

http://www.mathwire.com/geometry/tangrams.html

How to Do It

1. Look at and talk about the sizes and shapes of the tangram pieces. Count the pieces and name the shapes. (There are two large triangles, one medium triangle, two small triangles, one square, and one parallelogram in each set.)

2. Try making shapes or pictures by combining the tangram pieces. For each shape or picture, use all seven pieces.

Where Should I Go?

Give directions to find a hidden treasure, using words such as *above*, *under*, *over*, *around*, *behind*, *between*, and *through*, including *which way* and *how far to go*.

Great Books to Read Before Doing This Activity

Jonathan and His Mommy by Irene Smalls
Rosie's Walk by Pat Hutchins
Where Are You Going, Manyoni? by Catherine Stock

What's Needed

object to use as a hidden treasure

How to Do It

1. Talk with your child about why we need directions in order to find something. Ask, *Have you ever told someone how to get somewhere? What happens if we can't tell someone how to get to where they want to go?*

2. Hide the "treasure" while your child closes his eyes. When the treasure is hidden, give your child directions for finding the object.

3. As you give directions for finding the object, use as many positional, directional, shape, size, and number words as you can: *under, over, behind, next to, inside, go five steps back,* and so on.

4. Play the game several times, hiding the object in a different location each time, so your child has lots of opportunities to follow directions and find a treasure.

5. Now have your child hide the treasure and give you directions for finding it. If your child points and gives a vague direction such as, *Go over there,* you might say, *I can't see where you're pointing. Where should I go first? Can you tell me how to find it?*

It's easy to use positional and directional words with your child all day long: act out stories, talk about art projects, design and use treasure maps, or use them during scavenger hunts or in conversations about trips and transportation.

Obstacle Course

Build an obstacle course with your child, indoors or outdoors, and specify locations and describe spatial relationships—*near, under, over, behind, above, below, inside*—as you construct the obstacle course.

Great Books to Read Before Doing This Activity

Let's Try It Out with Towers and Bridges by Seymour Simon
Rosie's Walk by Pat Hutchins
Where Do I Live? by Neil Chesanow

What's Needed

blankets, sheets, or towels
cardboard boxes
cushions
furniture

How to Do It

1. Use a variety of available items to create a unique obstacle course for your child to climb through and explore. Obstacle courses are great for learning many ways of moving through space and learning words like *near, under, over, behind, above, below,* and *inside*.

2. Help your child set up the course, but make sure it will require words like *over, under, through, between, beside,* and so on.

3. To make a tunnel, place a blanket or large towel over the furniture, or set up two cardboard boxes near each other with another piece of cardboard serving as a roof.

4. As your child explores the obstacle course, talk with him about it: *You are under the blanket. I see you have crawled over the cushion. You went through the tunnel, and you came out beside the tree.*

Taking a Walk, Making a Map

Take a walk and draw a simple map that shows how to get from one place to another—you'll be communicating information and ideas by using drawings to express observations and experiences.

Great Books to Read Before Doing This Activity
Down the Road by Alice Schertle
Me on the Map by Joan Sweeney
Red Riding Hood by James Marshall

What's Needed
crayons or markers
large sheet of paper
Hint: Maps do not always have to be drawn on paper. Your child may enjoy creating maps with small blocks, Legos, or even clay or playdough.

How to Do It
1. Talk about maps. What does your child already know about maps? Explain that a map is a way of making a picture of a certain area, and that maps help us get from one place to another.
2. Take a short walk around your yard or neighborhood, and note all the things you see along the way.
3. As you walk, talk in detail about the route you are taking as you go: *First, we go out the door and onto the sidewalk. Next, we walk past a white house that's next to a green house, and then we see a brick house with a barking dog in the yard. There's a stop sign just around the corner.*

4. As you walk, make a list of things you see, encouraging your child to be as observant as possible. If your child misses something interesting, encourage him to look a little more closely. Also encourage your child to be specific in describing objects or landmarks.

5. When you get home from your walk, help your child draw a map showing where you went and what you saw. You can draw the line that shows the route, and your child can draw some of the things you saw along the way.

6. Read your map by demonstrating how to trace along the route with your finger while you tell each other where you went and what you saw.

7. Try making maps of different places: the route to school, to the library, or to a favorite friend's or relative's house.

8. Once your child becomes familiar with making maps, he may want to make them frequently. You might want to start collecting your child's maps in a homemade book and call it *My Atlas!*

Children learn how to get from one place to another, how to give and follow directions, and how to make and follow a map by doing the following:

- ▶ Observing and talking about landmarks,
- ▶ Constructing and understanding a route as a connected series of landmarks, and
- ▶ Putting many routes and locations together into a kind of mental map.

Make a Room Map

Together, make a map of one of the rooms in your house. Describe direction and distance as you talk about and represent objects and locations: *Where should it go? How far? Which way?*

Great Books to Read Before Doing This Activity

As the Crow Flies: A First Book of Maps by Gail Hartman
Me on the Map by Joan Sweeney
My Map Book by Sara Fanelli

What's Needed

crayons or markers
paper

How to Do It

1. On the paper, draw an outline of a room in your home.
2. Place drawings of furniture and other items on the map. You will need to use many positional words to place the objects in the right places: The refrigerator is *next to* the stove. The table is *in front of* the window.
3. Make maps of other places: your backyard, another room, or a playground.

> Simple maps are often included on brochures for campgrounds, amusement parks, or museums. When you take trips, include your child when you look at a map. He may not fully understand all of the markings on a map, but he will enjoy tracing the route with a finger.

3

Patterns and Relationships

Patterns and Relationships

When we think about math for young children, we often think about counting, writing numbers, and learning to add and subtract. While these skills are important, there are others, such as learning about patterns and relationships that help children learn to be strong mathematical thinkers.

Learning about patterns—things or events that repeat—helps children predict what will happen next, an important mathematical and life skill. Counting, for example, is a sequence. Whether you count forward or backward, by twos, fives, or tens, you have to know what comes next.

Whenever we say something is the *same as* or *different from* something else, we are trying to understand relationships by making comparisons using a single feature (color, shape, or size) or more than one characteristic (color *and* shape *and* size).

Here are some examples of how you and your child can explore patterns and sorting:

- ▶ Repeat a simple pattern as you build a tower of blocks that is red, green, yellow, red, green, yellow, and so on.
- ▶ Recognize and talk about patterns in your surroundings.
- ▶ Find and say repeated words and phrases in books.
- ▶ Copy each other's clapping or movement patterns.
- ▶ Notice and talk about how objects have similar or different characteristics.

- ▸ Sort collections of toys, laundry, and household objects in different ways by using different attributes.
- ▸ Sort game pieces by color before playing a game.
- ▸ Look at pictures of animals and make comparisons among them.

Books

Jonathan and His Mommy by Irene Smalls

Lots and Lots of Zebra Stripes by Stephen Swinburne

Max Found Two Sticks by Brian Pinkney

Pattern Bugs by Trudy Harris

Pattern Fish by Trudy Harris

Any picture book that has repeating themes, ideas, or language is a great way to discuss patterns with your child. Ask, *What happens next?* to prompt a discussion. When you introduce your child to a book for the first time, look at the cover together and wonder aloud, *What do you think this book will be about?*

Most of the world, both natural and human made, is constructed of units that repeat themselves in patterns. If you look closely at living things and human-made things, you will see many examples of simple repeating patterns, such as A-A-A-A; A-B, A-B; A-B-C, A-B-C; or A-A-B, A-A-B.

Music has rhythm and word patterns. Poetry is full of metrical patterns, and dance can have motion patterns.

Everyday Patterns

Create, copy, and extend patterns that you make with everyday objects.

Great Books to Read Before Doing This Activity

A Pair of Socks by Stuart J. Murphy
Pattern by Henry Arthur Pluckrose
Pattern Fish by Trudy Harris

What's Needed

collection of colored blocks, shapes, or other objects

How to Do It

1. Talk together about patterns—a sequenced or repeated organization of objects, sounds, or events. Here are some examples:

    ▶   Notice a pattern in a rug: *Look, our rug has a circle, then a flower, then a circle, then a flower...*

    ▶   Notice a pattern on a shirt: *My shirt has a striped pattern: green, blue, yellow, green, blue, yellow, green...*

    ▶   Talk about a daily routine (sequence of events): *Every day I do the same things: Get out of bed, take off my pajamas, get dressed, and eat breakfast.*

2. Continue your discussion of patterns by arranging the colored blocks or other objects in a repeating pattern.

    How would you describe the pattern? What comes next?
    Red, blue, red, blue, red, blue, red, blue, red... What comes next?
    Truck-bus-car, truck-bus-car, truck-bus-car, truck-bus... What comes next?
    Square-square-circle, square-square-circle, square... What comes next?

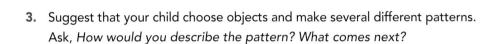

3. Suggest that your child choose objects and make several different patterns. Ask, *How would you describe the pattern? What comes next?*

4. Once your child understands how to make and identify a pattern, play Copy Cat Patterns. Take turns making, completing, and copying each other's patterns. Try to think of as many different patterns as possible.

Pattern Strips

Make pattern strips representing several different color patterns, and name and describe the patterns you create.

Great Books to Read Before Doing This Activity

A Pair of Socks by Stuart J. Murphy
Pattern by Henry Arthur Pluckrose
Pattern Fish by Trudy Harris

What's Needed

3" squares of different colors of construction paper
3" wide sheets of paper (one for each strip)
glue stick or tape

How to Do It

1. Select two different colored squares.

2. Talk with your child about the pattern: *I picked a red square, then a yellow square. Red, then yellow, then another red. What comes next in that pattern?*

3. Glue or tape the small squares to the base paper strip, continuing the pattern you started.

4. After your child becomes proficient with two colors, challenge him to select three colors and to make more patterns. How many different patterns can you make with three colors? Display or make a book of all your pattern strips.

Clapping and Tapping Patterns

Continue exploring patterns by copying and extending each other's clapping and tapping patterns.

Great Books to Read Before Doing This Activity
The Book of Tapping and Clapping by John Feierabend
Listen to the Rain by Bill Martin Jr. and John Archambault
Max Found Two Sticks by Brian Pinkney

What's Needed
colored blocks or shapes
your hands

How to Do It
1. Clap a simple rhythm for your child. Talk about the elements of the pattern, for example: one loud and two soft, or two fast and one loud. Clap the pattern again, and ask your child to repeat and then extend this pattern by asking, *What comes next?*
2. Take turns creating, repeating, and extending each other's clapping patterns.
3. Add tapping your head or another body part to your pattern:
   Tap head, tap knee, clap; tap head, tap knee, clap; tap head… What comes next?
4. Ask your child to create a new clapping pattern.

5. Use blocks or shapes to represent one of your clapping patterns. For example, one loud and two soft claps could be represented as one square and two triangles. Repeat this several times, and you have represented your pattern!

6. Try making and representing patterns with blocks or shapes first and then representing those patterns by clapping or tapping them together.

Sound Patterns

Explore sound patterns by tapping on a variety of objects and predicting what will come next in a simple pattern.

Great Books to Read Before Doing This Activity
The Book of Songs & Rhymes with Beat Motions by John Feierabend
Max Found Two Sticks by Brian Pinkney
Sounds All Around by Wendy Pfeffer

What's Needed
chopsticks or wooden spoons
table or other hard surface

How to Do It

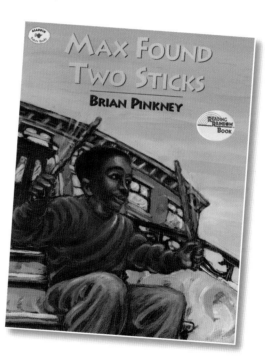

1. Tap a simple rhythm, which is a pattern, and have your child repeat it. Take turns tapping this simple pattern.

2. Have your child tap out a rhythm, and take turns tapping it out.

3. Try creating and repeating new and more complex rhythms by adding more taps and by mixing in a variety of fast and slow taps.

4. Can you and your child repeat the patterns you hear every day, such as the different patterns of rain on a window or roof, the ticking of a clock, or the sound of birdcalls?

Movement Patterns

Create, copy, and extend movement patterns.

Great Books to Read Before Doing This Activity
Baby Dance by Ann Taylor Clark
The Book of Songs & Rhymes with Beat Motions by John Feierabend
Drumbeat in Our Feet by Patricia A. Keeler and Julio Leitao
Jonathan and His Mommy by Irene Smalls

What's Needed
colored blocks or shapes
markers
paper

How to Do It
1. Help your child use blocks or shapes to create several different patterns.
2. Take turns representing the patterns with movements, for example:
   circle-square, circle-square could be represented by the following movements: hop-jump, hop-jump.

3. Have your child demonstrate a movement pattern and then challenge you to copy it with the blocks or shapes. Say the pattern together.

4. Show your child a movement pattern, and have her copy it with the blocks or shapes. Say the pattern together.

Pattern Dance

Put on some dance music, and invent a dance by combining two or three repeating patterns.

Great Books to Read Before Doing This Activity

Drumbeat in Our Feet by Patricia A. Keeler
Kitchen Dance by Maurie Manning
This Jazz Man by Karen Ehrhardt

What's Needed

music playing on a radio or on a recording
your bodies

How to Do It

1. Play some music that you and your child enjoy.
2. Make up a variety of movement patterns—sway your arms, take big and small steps, hop, and kick—to the beat of the music.
3. Invent a few movements, and ask your child to copy the pattern.
4. Ask your child to invent a pattern of movements, and copy her pattern.

Every day, we move in patterns. When we walk or run, sway to and fro to music, or even set the table, we are repeating a movement or a combination of movements.

Many games include movement and rhythm—following the steps to a dance, learning a skipping song, jumping rope, bouncing a ball and counting, or clapping to a song. Your child will love repeating these physical skills over and over in the process of learning and internalizing patterns of movement.

Combining movement and rhythm is a great way to learn because it's an active and fun way to internalize patterns. All of this helps your child recognize movement patterns in the world around her and adds to her understanding of the way things work.

Patterns All Around

Name and describe patterns you find in the world around you.

Great Books to Read Before Doing This Activity

Jonathan and His Mommy by Irene Smalls
Lots and Lots of Zebra Stripes by Stephen Swinburne
Stripes, Spots, or Diamonds by Patricia Stockland

What's Needed

books or magazines with lots of patterns (try design or home décor magazines)

How to Do It

1. Talk about patterns and then search for them in magazines and books. Remind your child that a pattern is something that repeats.
2. Look around the room and notice patterns. Ask questions such as:
    ▸ *What is one pattern we see in this room?*
    ▸ *How can we describe this pattern?*
    ▸ *What comes next in this pattern?*
3. Go on a pattern walk in your neighborhood, town, or park. On this walk, look for patterns everywhere: on buildings, in nature, on the ground, the sidewalk, and so on.
4. As you walk, stop and talk about the patterns you see, *How would you describe this pattern? What comes next in this pattern?*

5. Make some notes about the patterns you find. When you return home, talk about the patterns you found. You might want to suggest drawing them.

Pattern Border

Make pattern borders and designs with shape stamps made from sponges.

Great Books to Read Before Doing This Activity
A Pair of Socks by Stuart J. Murphy
Pattern Bugs by Trudy Harris
Pattern Fish by Trudy Harris

What's Needed
paper
scissors
sponge
tempera paint or inked stamp pad
tray or pan

How to Do It
1. Ask your child to pick the shape she would like the sponge stamp to be.
2. Use scissors (adult only) to cut the sponge into the shape your child chose.
3. Use an inked stamp pad or a little bit of tempera paint (poster paint) on a shallow tray or pan.
4. Help your child as needed to make pattern borders and designs on a piece of paper.
5. You can use the patterned paper for cards, invitations, or other decorations.

I Spy

Give clues about an object's characteristics using math vocabulary: size, shape, position, color, and so on.

Great Books to Read Before Doing This Activity
I See a Kookaburra! by Steve Jenkins
Seven Blind Mice by Ed Young
Who Is the Beast? by Keith Baker

What's Needed
descriptive words
good observation skills

How to Do It

1. Select an object in the room, but do not tell your child what it is. Say, *I spy something. . .*, then give a clue about the object. For example, if the object is a clock, you might say, *I spy something round.*

2. Ask your child to make a guess. She might ask, *Is it the lampshade?*

3. You answer no and give another clue. *I spy something round, and it is on the wall.*

4. Your child makes another guess. *Is it the mirror?*

5. You answer no and give another clue. *I spy something round. It is on the wall, and it has numbers on it.*

6. Your child then makes an informed guess. *Is it the clock?*

7. You say, *Yes! Now it's your turn to choose an object and give me clues!*

8. The most important part of this activity is giving good clues. Help your child come up with clues that describe shape, color, and other features of the object. Remind her not to say the name of the object when giving the

clues. Talk with your child about how the objects spied and the objects guessed are the same and different: The mirror is the same as the clock because both are on the wall, and both are round. They are different because the mirror shows us our reflections and the clock tells us what time it is.

It's in the Bag

Give clues about what is hidden in a feely bag.

Great Books to Read Before Doing This Activity

Is It Rough? Is It Smooth? Is It Shiny? by Tana Hoban
My Five Senses by Aliki
Opposites by Sandra Boynton

What's Needed

paper or fabric bag
small, familiar object, such as an orange

How to Do It

1. Select a familiar, small object (an orange, for example) from around your home.

2. Put the object in a bag without letting your child see it.

3. Have your child reach inside the bag, touch the object, and describe what she feels. She might guess that it's a ball.

4. Have your child continue to feel the object and make guesses until she figures out what the object is. You may want to give additional clues. *You can make juice from it.*

5. Take turns putting an object into the bag and being the guesser.

Sorting and More Sorting

Explore and sort collections of objects, looking for similarities and differences.

Great Books to Read Before Doing This Activity
Bein' with You This Way by W. Nikola-Lisa
Five Creatures by Emily Jenkins
Hannah's Collections by Marthe Jocelyn

What's Needed
collection of objects, such as toys, buttons, tools, socks, shoes, and other
    everyday objects
scissors
string or yarn

How to Do It
1. Look at, touch, and talk about the features of the different items in your collection.
2. Look for features that will help you sort the items: colors, shapes, sizes, types of material, and other features such as eyes, wheels, and so on.
3. Cut a long section of the string or yarn. Use this section to make a circle— this is your sorting loop.
4. Choose a feature to sort by. For example if you choose "all the toys with wheels," find the toys with wheels and put them in your sorting loop.
5. Take turns choosing a feature and sorting the objects by that feature. (This is also known as making a *set*.) As you and your child sort, talk about the feature you have chosen to create your set.

6. Make more sorting loops with the string or yarn.

7. Count and compare the sets you make. Ask questions such as the following:

   ▸ *Do you have more plastic toys or more wooden toys?*

   ▸ *How many toys do you have with wheels?*

   ▸ *How many are animals?*

   ▸ *Which set has the most?*

   ▸ *Which set has the fewest?*

   ▸ *Are there any objects that belong in two or more of our sets? Where shall we put them?*

8. Sort and re-sort the toys based on various features.

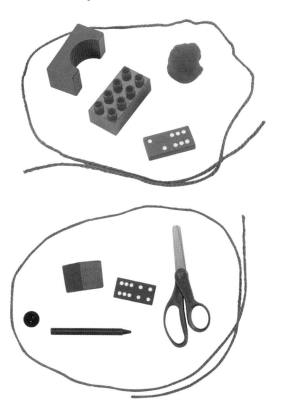

Sorting Tools

Look for similarities and differences, and sort a variety of tools.

Great Books to Read Before Doing This Activity

Albert's Alphabet by Leslie Tryon
Bunny Cakes by Rosemary Wells
Tool Book by Gail Gibbons

What's Needed

collection of tools, for example:

- ▶ drawing tools: pencil, crayon, and marker
- ▶ kitchen tools: spoon, measuring cup, small bowl, and whisk
- ▶ personal hygiene tools: hairbrush, toothbrush, and washcloth
- ▶ measuring tools: tape measure, ruler, and measuring cup

How to Do It

1. Gather a collection of tools, using the list on this page as a guide. Be sure that the items you choose are safe for your child to handle.

2. Allow your child plenty of time to sort the tools by their functions, such as tools used for writing, for cooking, for cleaning, and so on, or tools for measuring or mixing. Or sort the tools by which ones have numbers on them (measuring cups and a tape measure, for example), or group them by shape (the ruler is a rectangle; the spoon has an oval).

3. Talk with your child about the characteristics you are sorting by.

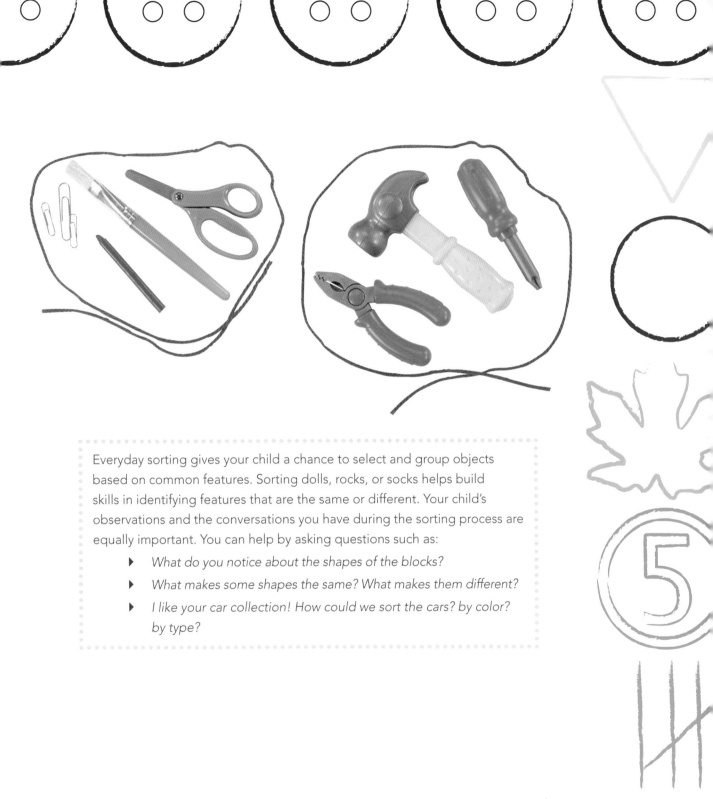

Everyday sorting gives your child a chance to select and group objects based on common features. Sorting dolls, rocks, or socks helps build skills in identifying features that are the same or different. Your child's observations and the conversations you have during the sorting process are equally important. You can help by asking questions such as:

▸ *What do you notice about the shapes of the blocks?*

▸ *What makes some shapes the same? What makes them different?*

▸ *I like your car collection! How could we sort the cars? by color? by type?*

Guess My Feature!

Create your own sorting collection and make a game of sorting by attribute.

Great Books to Read Before Doing This Activity

The Button Box by Margarette Reid
Hannah's Collections by Marthe Jocelyn
Hetty's 100 Hats by Janet Slingsby

What's Needed

everyday objects, such as blocks, bottle caps, cars, objects with two colors, objects with writing and numbers on them, shiny objects, small toy animals, things made of wood or metal or plastic, tools (paintbrush, comb, toothbrush, paper clip)

scissors

string or yarn

How to Do It

1. Explore the collection of objects. Look at, touch, and talk about the features of the different objects.

2. Describe some features that will help you sort the objects: color, shape, size, type of material, texture, and function. Talk about how the objects are the same and how they are different.

3. Cut a long section of string or yarn, and make a sorting loop.

4. Choose a feature to sort by (for example, all the red objects). Place these objects in a sorting loop.

5. When your set is complete, say, *Guess my feature!*

6. Help your child notice the features of your chosen set and make a guess about how you have sorted the objects: by color? by size? by shape? (Be patient, and ask leading questions if necessary. You may have to explain how you sorted the objects.)

7. When your child figures out how you sorted the objects, mix the collection up and take turns using a sorting loop to sort the collection by a "secret" feature.

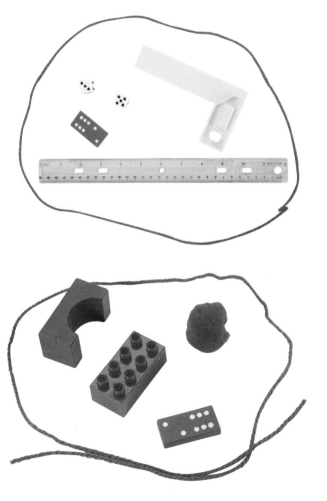

Nature Sort

Collect items from nature to sort and re-sort by a variety of features.

Great Books to Read Before Doing This Activity

If You Find a Rock by Peggy Christian
Let's Go Rock Collecting by Roma Gans
Seashells by the Seashore by Marianne Collins Berkes

What's Needed

natural items, such as shells, rocks, leaves, flowers, or pinecones

How to Do It

1. Go on a nature walk in your backyard or neighborhood with your child. Look for interesting items to collect.

2. When you return home, look at your collection. Talk with your child about what you have found, and help your child notice the features of the items: colors, sizes, shapes, and other characteristics.

3. Sort and re-sort your collection as you talk about features.

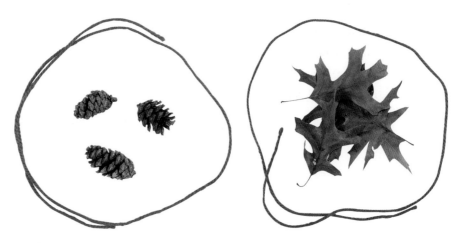

Sink or Float?

Investigate various objects and predict whether they will sink or float in water. Then, make a chart of your discoveries.

Great Books to Read Before Doing This Activity

Boats by Byron Barton
Mr. Gumpy's Outing by John Burningham
Who Sank the Boat? by Pamela Allen

What's Needed

markers
paper
small objects of various sizes, shapes, and materials: spoon, coin, bottle cap, canning lid, domino, and so on
water in a plastic tub or sink

How to Do It

1. Look at, touch, and describe each object:
   - *What is this object made of?*
   - *Is it big or little?*
   - *What is its shape?*
   - *What other characteristics do you notice?*
   - *Do you think it's a sinker or floater?*
2. Sort the objects into two groups: those you think will be "Sinkers" and those that will be "Floaters."

3. Test your predictions in the tub of water. Talk about similarities and differences between the sinkers and floaters:

☐ *What do you notice about the objects that sink?*

☐ *What do you notice about the objects that float?*

4. Make a chart on your paper, filling in the information about which objects sink and float. Are there some objects that float first, then sink? Create a category for those objects as well.

5. Talk with your child about the chart.

▶ *How are the sinkers the same or different from each other?*

▶ *How are the floaters the same or different from each other?*

Item	I predict...		What happened?	
	Sink	Float	Sank	Floated
penny				
paper clip				
block				

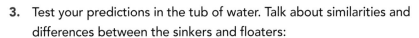

Sorting Every Day

Involve your child in the sorting you do every day.

Great Books to Read Before Doing This Activity

At the Supermarket by Anne Rockwell
Clean Your Room, Harvey Moon! by Pat Cummings
Hannah's Collections by Marthe Jocelyn

What's Needed

items that you need to sort: laundry, dishes, groceries, toys

How to Do It

1. Think about all the sorting you do every day: laundry, groceries, dishes, and toys.

2. Involve your child in helping you sort these household items. Identify and talk about how you are sorting: by colors, shapes, sizes, textures, or functions.

3. When you go to the grocery store together, talk about how different items are sorted and all the different features you see: all the cereal boxes are in the same section of the supermarket; all of the frozen food is stored in freezers in another section, and so on.

4. When you work together to clean up toys, talk about different ways to sort them: by type (cars, blocks, and so on), by color, by function (dolls and action figures, kitchen toys, toys with wheels), and so on.

What's a Minute?

Explore time and discover how long one minute is. Use math vocabulary such as *longer than*, *shorter than*, and *equal to*.

Great Books to Read Before Doing This Activity
10 Minutes till Bedtime by Peggy Rathmann
The Lion Book of Five-Minute Bedtime Stories by John Goodwin
Two-Minute Bedtime Stories by Elena Pasquali

What's Needed
one-minute timer
paper and marker for making your list

How to Do It
1. Talk about the word *minute*. Has your child ever heard that word? What does he think it means?

2. Look at and talk about the one-minute timer. This is a tool that shows just how long a minute lasts. Show your child how to read the timer to tell when a minute has passed.

3. Help your child understand how long a minute is by demonstrating an activity you can do for one minute: whistle, stand still, read a book, hop on one foot—anything you can easily do for that length of time.

4. Talk about activities you think you can do for more than a minute. Make a list of these predictions.

5. Now make a list of all the activities that might take less than a minute. Make a list of these predictions.

6. Test your suggestions by using the one-minute timer. Compare the results with your predictions.

4

Measuring and Comparing

Measuring and Comparing

Young children love to measure and make comparisons: They want to know how tall a skyscraper is, how much something weighs, who is tallest, who is shortest, how far it is to a certain place, or how much time an activity takes.

Whether it's size, weight, distance, or time, children naturally begin to explore measuring and comparing when they ask simple questions such as:

▶ *Is my tower taller than yours?*

▶ *Which tail is longer?*

▶ *Who's the shortest person in our family?*

Here are some examples of how you and your child can explore measurement:

▶ Use a variety of everyday items as measuring units (for example, your hand, a block, or a paper clip) to measure objects.

▶ Compare measurements and record your findings.

▶ Make good guesses or estimates about measurements.

▶ Use rulers, scales, thermometers, measuring cups, and clocks for exact measurements.

▶ Compare measurements, and describe things in terms of *longer than, shorter than, heavier than, lighter than, the same as,* and so on.

Books

A picture book such as *How Big Is a Foot?* by Rolf Myller is an enjoyable story about measurement that is fun for you and your child to read together. *Who Sank the Boat?* by Pamela Allen is a great call-and-response book about a group of friends on an outing—with a surprise ending. Your child will want to spend hours with *Actual Size* by Steve Jenkins, a book that explores measuring and making comparisons.

Here are a few more suggestions:

Actual Size by Steve Jenkins
How Big Is a Foot? by Rolf Myller
Inch by Inch by Leo Lionni
Twelve Snails to One Lizard by Susan Hightower

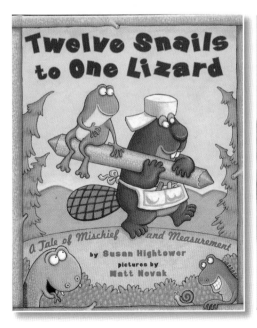

It's "MY Foot" Long

Use a nonstandard unit (an outline of your child's foot) to measure objects and distances.

Great Books to Read Before Doing This Activity

How Big Is a Foot? by Rolf Myller
Inch by Inch by Leo Lionni
Twelve Snails to One Lizard by Susan Hightower

What's Needed

marker
paper
scissors

How to Do It

1. Trace your child's foot onto a piece of paper. Cut out the tracing.
2. Select several objects in the room to measure: chair, table, book, and so on.
3. You might start by measuring the length of a table. Help your child place his foot tracing end to end on the table, counting the feet as you measure the length of the table. Record this number on a tally sheet.
4. Measure several other objects, counting and recording your measurements each time.
5. Look at your tally sheet and talk about what you observe:
   ▸ *Which object is the longest?*
   ▸ *Which object is the shortest?*
   ▸ *How do you know?*

6. For an added challenge, trace your foot on a piece of paper, and cut out the tracing. Compare the cutout of your foot with that of your child's: *Which is longer? Which is shorter?* Try measuring the same items you measured before, this time with your foot cutout. Record the measurements on your tally sheet. *How is each measurement different from the first measurement? Why?*

Item Measured	Actual # of 👣
chair	|||
table	||||
book		

How Tall Am I?

Measure each other and make comparisons, then communicate your findings.

Great Books to Read Before Doing This Activity

Actual Size by Steve Jenkins
How Long or How Wide? by Brian P. Cleary
Measuring Penny by Loreen Leedy

What's Needed

masking tape or painters' tape
nonstandard measuring units, such as chopsticks or liter bottles

How to Do It

1. Have your child lie on the floor while you place pieces of masking tape to mark both his head and his feet. When he stands up, talk about how long (tall) he is.

2. Hold up the object that will be used for measuring, such as a chopstick. Ask your child to estimate how many chopsticks will fit between the two pieces of tape on the floor. Help your child place chopsticks end to end from one piece of tape to the other. Count as you measure. How many chopsticks long is your child?

3. Now it's your turn to lie on the floor and have your child mark your length with masking tape.

4. Before measuring with the chopstick, ask your child to estimate how many chopsticks will fit between the two pieces of tape on the floor.

5. Help your child place chopsticks end to end from one piece of tape to the other. Count as you measure. How many chopsticks long are you?

Inching Along

Make your own measuring tool to measure objects in standard units (inches) and to compare lengths.

Great Books to Read Before Doing This Activity

How Big Is a Foot? by Rolf Myller
Inch by Inch by Leo Lionni
Ten Snails to One Lizard by Susan Hightower

What's Needed

one 12-inch chenille stick (also called a pipe cleaner)
collection of objects of different lengths
two drinking straws in two different colors
ruler
scissors
tape or glue

How to Do It

1. Using the ruler as a guide, cut the two different colored drinking straws into one-inch sections. You will need six sections of each color.

2. Help your child slide the straw sections onto the chenille stick in an alternating pattern. Tape the first piece of straw to one end of the chenille stick so the straw sections can't slide off as you add more. When all the sections are in place, tape the last one to the chenille stick, and you have created a flexible ruler for measuring in inches!

3. Encourage your child to use this ruler to measure all kinds of things: a table, chair, or person. After measuring lots of objects, have your child make comparisons. *Which is the longest object? Which is the shortest?*

When talking about measurements with your child, be sure to say the name of the unit. For example, when you ask your child how tall the table is, he may say, *Four*. Respond by asking, *Four what?* If your child has a hard time answering, give a prompt such as, *We used feet to measure, so the table is four feet tall.*

Longer than the Ruler

Make size comparisons as you measure items around your home.

Great Books to Read Before Doing This Activity

Great Estimations by Bruce Goldstone
How Tall, How Short, How Far Away
    by David A. Adler
Too Big, Too Small, Just Right by
    Frances Minters

What's Needed

flexible ruler from the Inching Along
    activity on pages 102–103
variety of household items

How to Do It

1. Using the flexible ruler you made in the Inching Along activity, challenge your child to find three things that look longer than the ruler, and then measure them to check. *Are they longer?*

2. Challenge your child to find three things that look shorter than the ruler and measure them. *Are they shorter?*

3. What other things would your child like to measure? Because the ruler is flexible, the objects do not have to be flat. *Can you find something the ruler can go around?*

Measure Me!

Use string to measure and compare the sizes of parts of your child's body—head, waist, arms, legs, and others.

Great Books to Read Before Doing This Activity
How Tall, How Short, How Far Away by David A. Adler
Measuring Penny by Loreen Leedy
Twelve Snails to One Lizard by Susan Hightower

What's Needed
nonstandard measurement units (dominoes, paper clips, clothespins, toothpicks, spoons, and so on)
paper
pencil
ruler or tape measure
scissors
string or yarn

How to Do It
1. Wrap a piece of string around your child's head and cut the string to that length.
2. Lay the piece of string flat on the table, and have your child guess how long the string is.
3. Have your child choose a nonstandard unit, such as dominoes, paper clips, or spoons, to measure the string. Help him measure the string by lining up the nonstandard units along the string. *How many dominoes does it take to go around your head? How many paper clips does it take?*

4. After measuring the string with the nonstandard units, you and your child can measure the string with a ruler or tape measure to find out how long it is in inches.

5. Help your child write both the nonstandard and standard head measurements on a simple chart.

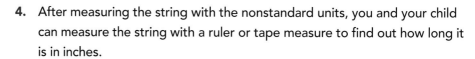

Body Part	Unit of Measurement	What I predict	Actual
head			
arm			
foot			

6. In the same way, measure around other parts of your child's body. You might try his chest, upper leg, or wrist. Ask what your child thinks. *Will these other body parts be bigger or smaller than your head?* Don't forget the guessing step!

Bigger than My Head

After your child has had practice measuring with the string, help her make some comparisons.

Great Books to Read Before Doing This Activity
Biggest, Fastest, Strongest by Steve Jenkins
Pig Pigger Piggest by Rick Walton
Size by Henry Arthur Pluckrose

What's Needed
string from Measure Me! on pages 107–108
variety of household items

How to Do It
1. Choose the size of one part of your child's body, such as the circumference of his head, to use as a nonstandard unit of measurement. (Use the string from the Measure Me! activity.)

2. With your child, look for things around the house that are shorter than, the same length as, and longer than the length of that string.

3. Try to guess the length of an object by using the string method of measuring. Have your child cut a piece of string that he thinks will go around something. For example, ask, *How long will the string need to be to go around your waist? Cut a piece that you think will be just right, and then we'll check it.*

Children love to learn new words—especially big words! Your child will enjoy learning the word *circumference*. The circumference is the distance around the outside edge of an object. *Let's put this string around the circumference of your head. When you say* circumference, *you sound just like a mathematician!*

Human Balance

Test the weights of various objects and compare them.

Great Books to Read Before Doing This Activity

Just a Little Bit by Ann Tompert
Weighing the Elephant by Ting-xing Ye
You Can Use a Balance by Linda Bullock

What's Needed

6–8 objects from around the house of different weights (each one should be
    light enough for your child to hold in one hand.) Examples could include a
    bar of soap, a book, a can of soup, a pencil, a stick of gum, or a tissue.
blindfold (if your child wants to use it)

How to Do It

Hint: The purpose of this activity is to help your child understand that *heavy*
and *light* are meaningful terms only when we are making comparisons. In
other words, the pebble is light when we compare it to a large rock, but the
pebble is heavy if we compare it to a feather.

1. Make a collection of objects to compare.
2. Have your child stand with his arms out straight and with hands turned
   palms-up.
3. Ask your child to close his eyes or to try wearing the blindfold if he would like.
4. Select two objects that have an obvious difference in weight. Place one
   object in your child's right hand and the other object in his left hand. (Your
   child is a human balance scale!)
5. Ask your child which object is heavier. Ask him to show this by lowering the
   hand with the heavy object while raising the hand with the lighter object.
6. Take turns being the human balance, with your "heavy" arm going lower
   and your "light" arm going higher.

Book of Opposites

Working together, make an opposites book about *heavy* and *light*.

Great Books to Read Before Doing This Activity

Eric Carle's Opposites by Eric Carle
Exactly the Opposite by Tana Hoban
Just a Little Bit by Ann Tompert

What's Needed

glue or tape
markers or crayons
old magazines
paper
scissors
stapler

How to Do It

1. Help your child find pictures in magazines or draw pictures that would show the concepts of *heavy* and *light.*

2. Help your child sort the pictures into pairs such that one item is *heavier* and the other item is *lighter.* Glue or tape each pair of pictures onto a separate piece of paper.

3. Write a caption for each picture. If the picture is of something *heavy*, the caption will be "A_____ is heavy." If the picture is of something *light*, the caption will be "A _____ is light."

4. Arrange the pages so that the left-hand side of the page shows items that are heavy and the right-hand side of the page shows items that are light.

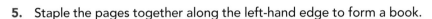

5. Staple the pages together along the left-hand edge to form a book.

6. Let your child make a cover for the book by pasting or drawing pictures of things of different weights.

7. You can make the book more challenging by putting three pictures on each page. The picture in the middle might be a horse. On one side of the horse, there might be a cat. On the other side of the horse there might be a whale. Your child might say, *A horse is heavier than a cat and lighter than a whale.*

A bookcase is heavy.

A doll is light.

When you and your child use the words *heavy* and *light*, make sure you explain what those words mean. You might ask your child, *What does* heavy *mean?* He might need help expressing the meaning clearly, so you might have to say, Heavy *means that something weighs more than something else.* Light *means that something weighs less than something else.*

Also, use the word *compare*. When we use words like *heavy* and *light*, we are always making a comparison. You might ask, *What would be* light *when compared to your teddy bear?*

What would be heavy?

Make a Balance Mobile

Make a simple mobile that will act as a balance, then use math vocabulary such as *heavier than*, *lighter than*, and *equal to* to describe the relative weights of a few objects.

Great Books to Read Before Doing This Activity

The 100-Pound Problem by Jennifer Dussling
Just a Little Bit by Ann Tompert
You Can Use a Balance by Linda Bullock

What's Needed

6–8 small objects (pebble, nut in the shell, small toy car, crayon or marker, comb, toothbrush, Lego piece, and so on)
scissors
stick of wood 2–3 feet long (Help your child use his measuring skills!)
string or yarn

How to Do It

1. Talk together about *weight* and *balance*. Ask your child, *Have you ever seen a seesaw at the playground?* Explain that for a seesaw to balance, the two people on the seesaw have to be about the same weight. The two sides of the seesaw have to be *balanced*.

2. Working together, make a balance mobile that you can use to experiment with weight and balance.

3. Tie a piece of string or yarn to the center of the stick and hang the stick where it will hang freely and both you and your child can reach it easily—on the back of a chair, from a floor lamp, from the end of a counter. Find just the right spot on the stick to tie the string so the stick is balanced. It should hang evenly.

4. Help your child pick two objects from the collection that weigh about the same.

5. Tie strings to the objects, and tie one onto each end of the stick. If they do not balance right away, challenge your child to figure out what he can do to make them balance. (Changing the length of the string or sliding one object toward the center of the stick will affect the balance, but see if your child can figure this out!)

   Hint: This activity also works with a clothes hanger. Attach a piece of string to the hook on the hanger to hang it somewhere as you balance your objects.

6. Once you get these first two objects to balance, try adding two more. Hang them beside the first two objects or from the bottoms of the first two objects. Now the Balance Mobile may look like this:

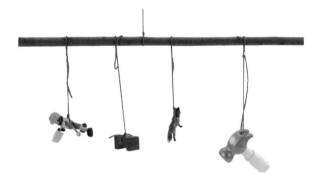

7. It will be harder and harder to balance the mobile as you try to add more objects. See how many objects you can hang before it gets too hard to find the balance point.

Another Simple Balance

Make a very simple beam balance with a ruler and a domino, and use this tool to compare the weights of small objects.

Great Books to Read Before Doing This Activity
The 100-Pound Problem by Jennifer Dussling
Just a Little Bit by Ann Tompert
You Can Use a Balance by Linda Bullock

What's Needed
domino
ruler
small objects, such as paper clips, crackers, or pennies

How to Do It
1. Place the domino on its long, thin edge, and set the ruler on it, balanced in the center.
2. Have your child place small objects such as paper clips, crackers, or pennies on each end of the ruler to find different combinations of things that weigh the same and balance each other.
3. Talk with your child as you observe and describe the results of your experiments. Use the terms *heavier than*, *lighter than*, and *equal to*.

What Do You Do First?

Act out the sequences of daily routines and activities, and use math vocabulary such as *first*, *second*, and *third*.

Great Books to Read Before Doing This Activity

10 Minutes till Bedtime by Peggy Rathmann
Froggy Gets Dressed by Jonathan London
The Little Red Hen (Makes a Pizza) by Philemon Sturges

What's Needed

Objects to help you act out your routines (optional)

How to Do It

1. Talk together about your daily routines and activities: getting ready for bed, dressing, getting ready to go somewhere, preparing for a trip, cooking a meal, and so on.

2. Start with a bedtime routine. Ask your child:
    - *What do we do first?*
    - *What do we do next?*
    - *What is the third thing we do?*

3. Discuss each part of the routine. What simple motion or action could you use to demonstrate each part of the sequence?

4. Take turns acting out your child's bedtime routine: using the bathroom, taking a bath, brushing teeth, changing into pajamas, getting a drink, getting into bed, reading a story, kissing goodnight, and going to sleep.

5. Now take turns acting out your bedtime routine. How are your routines the same? How are they different?

6. Talk about other activities that are done in a sequence: cooking, dressing—what else?

7. Stories have a sequence. After reading a book several times, talk about the sequence of events in the story.

Mathematics Standards

Bibliography Index

Math Standards

The information and activities in *How Many Ways Can You Make Five?* are based on the National Council of Teachers of Mathematics (NCTM) *Principles and Standards for School Mathematics, PreK-Grade 2,* and the *Common Core State Standards Initiative*. NCTM identifies ten areas that cover a broad range of math skills and understandings—five are identified as process standards and five as content standards.

We use the processes and skills of mathematics every day because they help us explore the world in a meaningful way. This list of standards is a handy reference tool to use as you explore this book. Consider reviewing the standards every once in a while, after doing some activities with your child. You'll be surprised at how many skills and concepts you use every single day!

The Process Standards

Problem Solving
Using simple approaches to solving mathematical problems: asking for help, counting, trial and error, guessing and checking

Reasoning and Proof
Learning to explain how a mathematical problem is solved: describing the steps taken, verbally, in a drawing, or with concrete objects

Communicating
- Telling others about her math-related work: using language, pictures or other symbols, or concrete objects
- Beginning to use math language: number names, shape names, size words, names of math materials, and so on

Making Connections

▸ Using math skills in a variety of situations, not just when prompted by an adult

▸ Linking his or her own math experiences to those of other people, in real life or in books

▸ Recalling previous math experiences when engaged in current ones

Representing

▸ Using simple pictures, graphs, diagrams, or dictated words to represent mathematical ideas

The Content Standards

Numbers and Operations

▸ Recognizing and naming some written numerals

▸ Having a sense of quantity: Knowing that the number name *three* and the symbol *3* mean three of something

▸ Counting: Learning the sequence of number names (*1, 2, 3*)

▸ Counting objects: Learning to count an object only once, using one-to-one correspondence in counting objects, and matching groups of objects

▸ Beginning addition: Adding two groups of objects by counting the total

▸ Beginning subtraction: Taking away one group of objects from another and counting the remainder

▸ Comparing: Understanding ideas such as *more than*, *less than*, and *the same as*, and having a general idea that some numbers mean *a lot* and some numbers mean a *few*

Geometry and Spatial Sense

▶ Matching, sorting, naming, and describing shapes: circles, squares, rectangles, and triangles

▶ Naming and describing shapes found in everyday environments

▶ Combining shapes to make new shapes

▶ Making shape designs that have symmetry and balance

▶ Understanding and using words that describe where objects are located: *over, under, through, above, below, beside, behind, near, far, inside, outside*

Patterns, Relationships, Functions, and Algebra

▶ Identifying, making, copying, and extending simple patterns: sequenced or repeated organization of objects, sounds, or events

▶ Using patterns to predict what will come next in a sequence

▶ Recognizing single-number patterns such as "one more"

▶ Noticing, describing, and explaining mathematical changes in quantity, size, temperature, or weight

▶ Sorting a group or groups of objects based on common attributes (characteristics)

Measurement

▶ Understanding and using words referring to quantities: *big, little, tall, short, long, a lot, a little, hot, cold, heavy, light*

▶ Understanding and using comparative words: *more than, less than, bigger than, smaller than, shorter than, longer than, heavier than, colder than*

▶ Showing an awareness of and interest in measuring: imitating the use of measuring tools and measuring with nonstandard units

▶ Comparing objects: *Which of these two sticks is longer?*

▶ Beginning to use measurement words, such as *inches, feet, miles, pounds, minutes,* and *hours*

Data Analysis, Statistics, and Probability

▶ Sorting objects to answer questions

▶ Collecting data to answer a question: keeping track of simple information gathered from a group of people or over a short length of time

▶ Making lists or basic graphs, with adult help, to organize collected data

Bibliography

This bibliography contains children's books recommended for the math themes addressed in this book, but it's just a start! Our online database is updated frequently as new books are published. Please search www.mothergooseprograms.org to find the newest titles. For out-of-print books, please check with your local library.

Much More than Counting: Numbers and Operations

1, 2, Buckle My Shoe by Anna Grossnickle Hines
Take cloth and buttons and thread. Add a classic nursery rhyme and a counting game. Stitch them together, and what do you have? A patchwork of numbers and fun!

10 Minutes till Bedtime by Peggy Rathmann
What the humans at 1 Hoppin Place do not know is that their cherished family pet hamster has advertised on the Web (www.hamstertours.com) for a "10-Minute Bedtime Tour," and the hordes have only just begun to descend.

12 Ways to Get to 11 by Eve Merriam
Go on an adventure with this innovative counting book.

The Doorbell Rang by Pat Hutchins
Ma gives Sam and Victoria a dozen cookies to share—plenty for two children. But then, the doorbell rings and rings and rings as more children arrive to share the cookies. Finally, each child has just one cookie. What happens next?

How Do You Count a Dozen Ducklings? by In Seon Chae
A mama duck with a dozen eggs has to do a lot of counting! Mama counts her ducklings one by one as they hatch, but soon she finds clever new ways to count to twelve: by twos, threes, fours, and sixes! But how many ducklings will it take to trick the hungry wolf who is counting on them for lunch?

How Many, How Many, How Many by Rick Walton
The reader counts from one to twelve while guessing the answers to questions about nursery rhymes, names of the seasons, players on a football team, and other basic information.

One Duck Stuck by Phyllis Root
Different marshland creatures offer to help one duck stuck in the muck.

One Hundred Hungry Ants by Elinor Pinczes
One hundred ants march toward a picnic, and the littlest ant decides he would like to step up the pace.

Seven Blind Mice by Ed Young
One by one, seven blind mice investigate the strange Something by the pond. What is it?

Ten, Nine, Eight by Molly Bang
A counting lullaby showing the room of a little girl who is going to bed.

Shapes and Spaces

Grandfather Tang's Story by Ann Tompert
This original tangram tale is framed by the loving relationship between a grandfather and a granddaughter as they share the story under the shade of an old tree.

I Spy Shapes in Art by Lucy Micklethwait
This book presents shapes to find in paintings by such artists as Winslow Homer, Georgia O'Keeffe, Paul Klee, and Henri Matisse.

Mouse Shapes by Ellen Stoll Walsh
What can you make with one oval, two circles, and eight triangles? Just ask three clever mice—who even find a funny way to trick a sneaky cat.

Orange Pear Apple Bear by Emily Gravett
A plump bear adds a humorous touch to this charming book about shapes, colors, and sequence.

The Quilting Bee by Gail Gibbons
A quilting circle, consisting of adults and two child helpers, plans a new quilt to display at the county fair. Readers learn how quilts are made and discover their fascinating history as well as lots of fun facts.

The Shape of Things by Dayle Ann Dodds
Simple rhymes and bold illustrations help youngsters learn to see and, eventually, to draw the world around them.

Shapes, Shapes, Shapes by Tana Hoban
A wordless picture book that encourages children to find shapes.

A Star in My Orange by Dana Rau
Rau looks to nature for inspiration and finds stars, not just in the sky but in an orange half, a starfish, and a snowflake. She sees spirals in a seahorse, a ram's horn, and a seashell. A very simple yet effective book presenting fundamental forms children can observe in nature.

Maps and Mapping

As the Crow Flies: A First Book of Maps by Gail Hartman
An exploration of map skills used to follow the paths of several animals.

Down the Road by Alice Schertle
Hetty is very careful with the eggs she has bought on her very first trip to the store, but she runs into trouble when she stops to pick apples.

Mapping Penny's World by Loreen Leedy
A girl maps her bedroom and her dog Penny's world.

Me on the Map by Joan Sweeney
A young girl introduces the world of mapmaking. She begins with the floor plans of her room and house and then expands from home to street to town to state to country and, finally, to the world.

My Map Book by Sara Fanelli
A collection of maps provides views of the owner's bedroom, school, playground, and other realms farther away.

Rosie's Walk by Pat Hutchins
The fox is after Rosie, but Rosie does not know it. She leads him on a long walk into one disaster after another, each one more fun than the last.

Where Are You Going, Manyoni? by Catherine Stock
A child living near the Limpopo River in Zimbabwe encounters several wild animals on her long walk to school.

Patterns

Jonathan and His Mommy by Irene Smalls
As a mother and son explore their neighborhood, they try various ways of walking.

Lots and Lots of Zebra Stripes by Stephen Swinburne
The author defines *patterns* as "lines and shapes that repeat" and finds these patterns everywhere.

Max Found Two Sticks by Brian Pinkney
Although he doesn't feel like talking, Max responds to questions by drumming on various objects.

Pattern by Henry Pluckrose
Large, colorful photos of everyday things help reinforce the text in this fun, easy introduction to the concept of patterns.

Pattern Fish by Trudy Harris
A fun look at patterns.

Sounds All Around by Wendy Pfeffer
Clap your hands, snap your fingers: You're making sounds! Find out how people and animals use different kinds of sound to communicate.

The Three Bears by Paul Galdone
This and many of the other classic folktales illustrate patterns in language and size.

Sorting

Bein' with You This Way by W. Nikola-Lisa
A rap poem with rich, catchy phrases that celebrate diversity.

The Button Box by Margarette Reid
A little boy explores his grandmother's button box.

Five Creatures by Emily Jenkins
A girl describes the three humans and two cats who live in her house, and details some shared traits.

Hannah's Collections by Marthe Jocelyn
Hannah has a challenge: Which of her many collections should she choose to share with her class?

Is It Rough? Is It Smooth? Is It Shiny? by Tana Hoban
Color photographs introduce objects of many different textures.

Let's Go Rock Collecting by Roma Gans
Readers follow two rock hounds around the globe as they add to their collection.

Seashells by the Seashore by Marianne Berkes
Sue walks the shore, collecting seashells for her grandmother's birthday.

Sorting by Henry Pluckrose
Uses everyday objects to introduce the concept of sorting.

Tool Book by Gail Gibbons
This book shows tools used in building and describes what they are used for.

Measurement

Actual Size by Steve Jenkins
How big is a crocodile? Can you imagine a two-foot-long tongue? Sometimes facts and figures don't tell the whole story. Sometimes you need to see things for yourself—at their actual size.

Biggest, Strongest, Fastest by Steve Jenkins
An informative introduction to the "world records" held by fourteen members of the animal kingdom.

Great Estimations by Bruce Goldstone
If someone handed you a big bowl of jelly beans, how would you figure out how many there are? You could count them, one by one, or you could estimate. This unique book will show you how to train your eyes and your mind to make really great estimates.

How Big Is a Foot? by Rolf Myller
The king wants to give the queen something special for her birthday. The queen has everything—everything except a bed. The trouble is that no one in the kingdom knows the answer to a very important question: How big is a bed? (Here's the catch: beds have not yet been invented!)

Inch by Inch by Leo Leonni
A story of an inchworm who measures his way out of being eaten by a bird.

Just a Little Bit by Ann Tompert
When Elephant and Mouse try to play on a seesaw, they need help from a vast number of animal friends to balance the scales.

Measuring Penny by Loreen Leedy
For homework, Lisa measures her dog, Penny. She uses standard and nonstandard measures.

Twelve Snails to One Lizard by Susan Hightower
A silly story about inches, feet, and yards.

Index

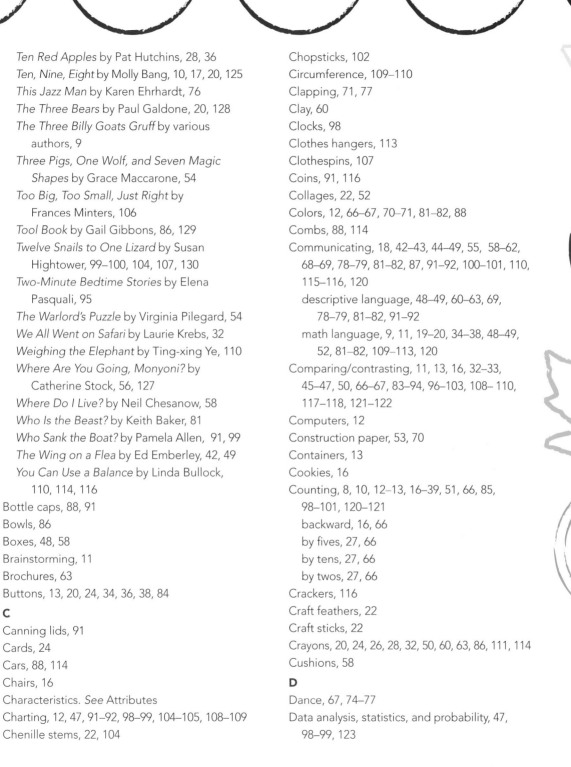

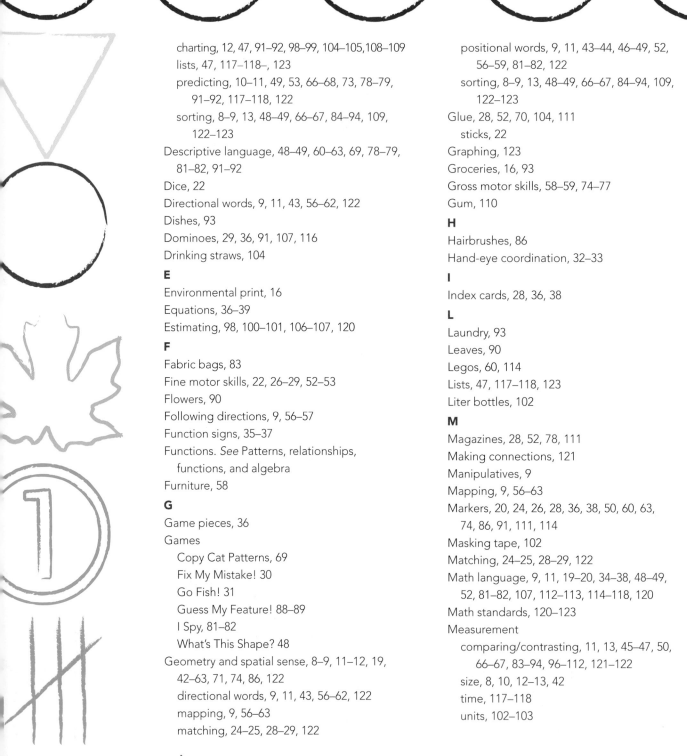

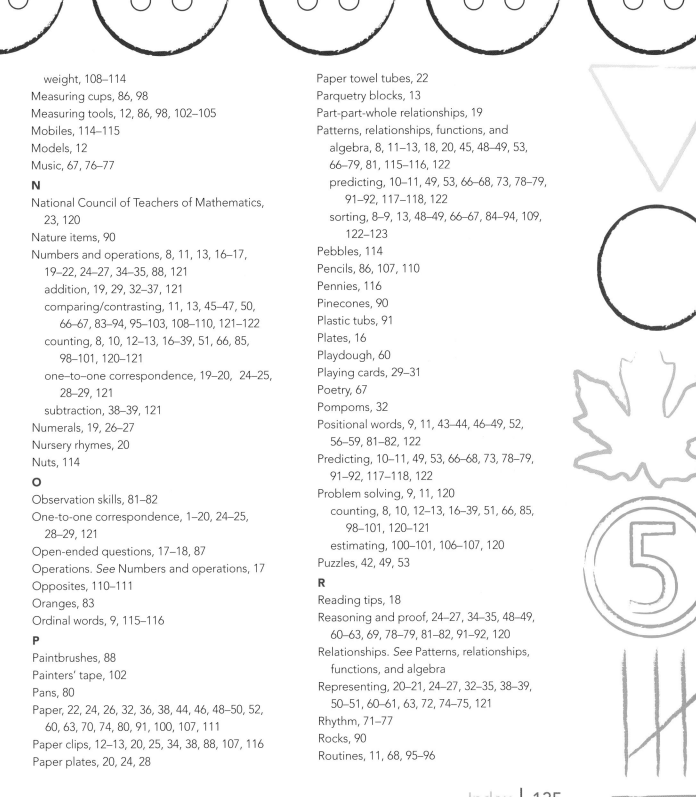

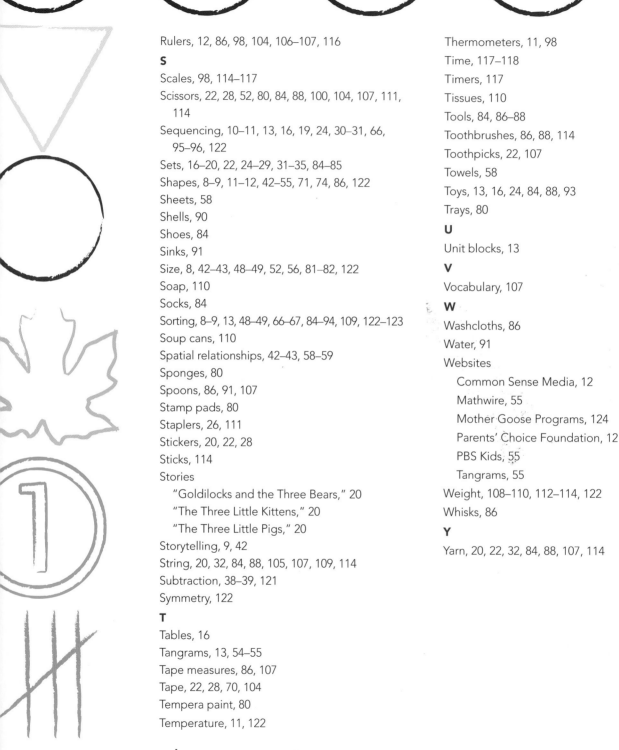